Supercarriers

by Michael Burgan

CAPSTONE
HIGH-INTEREST
BOOKS

an imprint of Capstone Press
Mankato, Minnesota

Capstone High-Interest Books are published by Capstone Press
151 Good Counsel Drive, P.O. Box 669, Mankato, Minnesota 56002
http://www.capstone-press.com

Library of Congress Cataloging-in-Publication Data
Burgan, Michael.
    Supercarriers/by Michael Burgan.
    p. cm.—(Land and sea)
    Includes bibliographical references (p. 45) and index.
    ISBN 0-7368-0760-8
    1. Aircraft carriers—United States—Juvenile literature. [1. Aircraft carriers.]
I. Title. II. Land and sea (Mankato, Minn.)
V874.3. B87 2001
359.9'4835'0973—dc21   00-009828

Summary: Describes the history, design, weapons, and missions of supercarriers.

Editorial Credits
Carrie A. Braulick, editor; James Franklin, cover designer; Timothy Halldin,
    production designer and illustrator; Katy Kudela, photo researcher

Photo Credits
Defense Visual Information Center, 10
Photri-Microstock, cover, 4, 6, 8, 13, 14, 17, 21, 22, 24, 27, 30, 32, 34, 36, 40, 42
Unicorn Stock Photos/Joe Sohm, 18
William B. Folsom, 39

1 2 3 4 5 6 06 05 04 03 02 01

**Special thanks to David Waterman of the Navy Office of Information–East for his
assistance in preparing this book.**

Table of Contents

Chapter One

Supercarriers

The U.S. Navy uses many types of warships. These ships are equipped with weapons such as guns and missiles. Aircraft carriers are one type of warship. These ships are designed to carry helicopters and airplanes. Pilots can take off from and land on the ships. Aircraft carriers also are called carriers.

The largest aircraft carriers are called supercarriers. These carriers are the world's largest warships.

About Supercarriers
Supercarriers carry many aircraft and crewmembers. They can hold more than 80 aircraft. Most supercarriers can carry more

Supercarriers are the world's largest warships.

Supercarriers carry F/A-18 Hornets.

than 6,000 sailors. These sailors are trained to operate and maintain the ship. An air wing also is aboard each supercarrier. An air wing includes aircraft, pilots, and technicians. Technicians are trained to maintain and repair aircraft.

A supercarrier's main body is called the hull. The ship's bow is located at the hull's front. Its stern is located at the hull's rear.

Each supercarrier travels with other warships such as frigates and destroyers. Frigates and destroyers are small, fast warships equipped with many weapons. They help defend the carrier from enemy attacks. Together, the carrier and ships make up a battle group.

Most supercarriers are powered by nuclear reactors instead of an oil-burning engine. Reactors are large machines that produce nuclear energy. Reactors are smaller, cleaner, and use less energy than oil-burning engines. Reactors' energy supply lasts for more than 20 years. Ships powered by oil-burning engines need the crew to regularly add fuel. Reactors allow supercarriers to remain at sea for long periods of time.

Supercarrier Aircraft

An aircraft carrier's main weapons are its aircraft. These planes attack enemy ships and aircraft that approach the battle group.

Supercarriers have two kinds of fighter planes. These planes are F-14 Tomcats and F/A-18 Hornets. They are designed to shoot down enemy planes.

Supercarriers also have E-2C Hawkeyes. Crewmembers search for enemy ships and planes with Hawkeyes. These planes carry

EA-6B Prowlers send out electronic signals to shut down enemy radar.

radar equipment that uses radio waves to locate distant objects.

Supercarriers carry EA-6B Prowlers. These planes send out electronic signals to shut down enemy radar. Prowlers also fire missiles at enemy targets.

Supercarriers also have two types of aircraft that hunt submarines. They are S-3B Viking planes and SH-60F Oceanhawk helicopters. These aircraft have advanced radar

and communications equipment to locate enemy submarines.

Supercarrier Missions

The Navy uses supercarriers for various missions. The Navy sails battle groups near countries that threaten to attack the United States or its allies. These countries are friendly with the United States. This action is called "showing the flag." The threatening countries often choose not to fight when they see the U.S. battle group.

Some supercarrier battle groups perform patrol missions. If a battle begins, the closest battle group on patrol can quickly reach the combat area.

Supercarrier planes fly missions to shoot down enemy planes. The carrier planes also can drop bombs on enemy weapons or bases.

Supercarrier battle groups are able to form blockades. They prevent ships from leaving or entering a port. Battle groups sometimes form blockades to prevent enemies from receiving important supplies.

Chapter Two

History

The U.S., British, and French Navies began testing ideas for carriers in the early 1900s. In 1910, an American pilot named Eugene Ely flew a plane off a ship for the first time. Ely also landed a plane on a ship that year. These feats proved that aircraft carriers could be useful to the world's navies.

The First Carriers

The first U.S. Navy aircraft carrier was called the *Langley*. It was built in 1922. The Navy added a flight deck to an existing ship. The flight deck is the main level of an aircraft carrier. Pilots take off and land on the flight deck.

The *Langley* was the Navy's first aircraft carrier.

In 1927, the Navy commissioned two aircraft carriers called the *Saratoga* and the *Lexington*. Commissioned ships are in active service.

World War II

The Navy built several carriers during World War II (1939–1945). The Navy had more than 90 commissioned aircraft carriers by the war's end. The Navy grouped these carriers into separate classes. All Navy ships in a class share certain features such as length and speed. They also perform the same types of missions.

The Allied nations fought against the Axis powers during World War II. The Allied nations included the United States, Great Britain, the Soviet Union, Canada, and France. The Axis powers included Germany, Italy, and Japan.

The Japanese controlled many islands in the Pacific Ocean during the war. Planes from U.S. carriers attacked Japanese troops on the islands. The planes also attacked Japanese ships.

The *Saratoga* was commissioned in 1927.

In the late 1940s, the Navy began using planes with jet engines. These planes burn fuel to create exhaust gases. The gases rush out a jet plane's rear and cause it to move forward. Previous planes had engines with pistons. These circular metal pieces move up and down to create power. Jet planes were heavier and more powerful than other aircraft. Many of the Navy's

carriers could not support the weight of jet planes.

United States

In 1949, the Navy started to build a large aircraft carrier that could launch jet planes. This carrier was called *United States*. But the ship's construction ended within a few days. Some military leaders decided the country could not afford to build such a large carrier. They also believed that aircraft carriers would not play a major role in future wars.

In 1950, North Korea invaded South Korea. This action began the Korean War (1950–1953). The United States fought alongside South Korea during this war. Aircraft carriers arrived quickly at battle sites. The carriers' planes were successful during the battles. The U.S. government then realized that aircraft carriers were important to the country's military.

A supercarrier's aircraft can quickly reach mission sites.

Forrestal

In 1952, the Navy began to build another large carrier to carry jet planes. This ship was called the *Forrestal*. It was commissioned in 1955.

The *Forrestal* was designed to be smaller than the *United States*. But the ship was still larger than previous U.S. carriers. The *Forrestal* was about 1,046 feet (319 meters) long. It had a displacement of about 80,000 tons (72,600 metric tons). People use displacement to measure a ship's weight. Displacement is the weight of the water that would fill up the space taken up by the ship. At the time, the largest carriers were about 900 feet (275 meters) long and had a displacement of about 60,000 tons (54,400 metric tons).

The *Forrestal* traveled at about the same speed as previous carriers. Its top speed was more than 30 knots. One knot equals about 1.15 miles (1.85 kilometers) per hour.

The *Forrestal's* flight deck was different from those of previous carriers. The *Forrestal* had a

The *Forrestal* was large enough to carry jet engine planes.

longer flight deck than older carriers. Jet engine planes need more space to take off and land.

The *Forrestal's* flight deck also had two runway systems. One runway was slanted away from the other. These runways allowed planes to take off and land at the same time. Previous carriers had only one runway.

The *Forrestal* had four catapults. These pieces of equipment launch aircraft off carriers. Other carriers had only two catapults. The

The Navy commissioned *John F. Kennedy* in 1968.

Forrestal's catapults used steam power to launch aircraft. Previous carriers used hydraulic catapults. Steam-powered catapults were more powerful than hydraulic catapults.

Before 1960, the Navy built three other ships similar to the *Forrestal*. These ships became part of the *Forrestal* class.

In the early 1960s, the Navy began to classify carriers. Carriers that could carry jet planes were called attack aircraft carriers. Many people began to call these larger carriers "supercarriers." Other carriers were not designed to carry jet planes. The Navy classified these ships as anti-submarine warfare support aircraft carriers.

Kitty Hawk

In 1961, the Navy commissioned the first two supercarriers in the *Kitty Hawk* class. It later built another *Kitty Hawk*-class carrier.

Kitty Hawk carriers are 1,062 feet (324 meters) long and have a displacement of about 81,000 tons (73,500 metric tons). The Navy still uses *Kitty Hawk* carriers today.

Enterprise and John F. Kennedy

In 1961, the Navy also commissioned the *Enterprise*. The *Enterprise* is the world's first carrier to operate on nuclear power. It is 1,123 feet (342 meters) long and has a displacement of 89,600 tons (81,285 metric tons).

In 1965, pilots flew planes off the *Enterprise* during the Vietnam War (1954–1975). North Vietnam fought against South Vietnam during this war. The United States fought alongside South Vietnam. Pilots from the *Enterprise* were able to quickly arrive at battle areas. The Navy still uses the *Enterprise* today.

In 1968, the Navy commissioned *John F. Kennedy*. This supercarrier is in its own class. *John F. Kennedy* is about 1,052 feet (320 meters) long. It has a displacement of about 61,000 tons (55,300 metric tons). *John F. Kennedy* is still in active service today.

Nimitz

In 1975, the Navy commissioned a new type of nuclear-powered supercarrier. This carrier was called the *Nimitz*. The *Nimitz* was the first ship in a new class of supercarriers. *Nimitz*-class supercarriers are the world's largest warships.

The Navy currently has eight *Nimitz*-class supercarriers and plans to commission more in the future. These carriers are 1,092 feet (333 meters) long. Their flight decks are 252 feet (77 meters) wide. *Nimitz*-class carriers have a displacement of about 97,000 tons (88,000 metric tons).

Nimitz-class carriers are the world's largest supercarriers.

The Navy used *Nimitz*-class carriers in the Gulf War (1991). This war began when Iraq invaded Kuwait. The carriers were located in the Persian Gulf. This large body of water is near Kuwait. The U.S. military helped defend Kuwait from Iraq. Planes from *Nimitz*-class carriers fought successful battles against the Iraqi military.

Nimitz carriers often patrol to assist in combat duties if they are needed. Since 1991, the Navy has sent *Nimitz*-class carriers to the Persian Gulf to patrol.

Nimitz-class carriers often patrol the world's oceans.

On Board a Supercarrier

Some people call supercarriers "cities at sea." The ships can sail for months at a time. Supercarriers hold all aircraft maintenance equipment such as fuel and spare parts. They also carry ship parts and weapons.

Decks

All large ships have levels called decks. The island is located on the flight deck. A carrier's captain and other crewmembers control the ship from the island. Trained sailors on the island use radios to tell pilots when to take off and land. This communication helps pilots

Supercarriers carry weapons such as missiles.

avoid accidents. Radar equipment is located on top of the island.

The hangar bay is below the flight deck. Aircraft is stored on this level. Technicians also repair aircraft on the hangar bay. Large elevators take the aircraft from the hangar bay to the flight deck.

The mess deck is below the hangar bay. The main eating area is on this deck. Most crewmembers live on decks below the mess deck. These decks have small living areas called compartments. Each compartment holds many beds called racks.

Takeoff and Landing Gear

Modern supercarriers have four catapults to launch aircraft. Each catapult is about 300 feet (90 meters) long. Aircraft launched from a catapult can reach speeds of more than 160 miles (257 kilometers) per hour in two seconds.

Carriers have special equipment to help aircraft land. Four steel wires called arresting wires stretch across the flight deck. Each plane

Aircraft is stored on the hangar bay.

has a hook attached to its tail. Pilots use this hook to grab onto one of the arresting wires. The arresting wire then stops the plane. Pilots sometimes miss the wires. They then must circle around the ship to try catching a wire again.

Nuclear Power

Nuclear reactors are located in the center of the ship's lowest deck. *Nimitz*-class supercarriers have two nuclear reactors. The *Enterprise* has eight nuclear reactors.

Rods made of a metal called uranium lie inside the reactors. Atoms in the uranium split apart to release energy. Atoms are extremely small pieces of matter. Uranium atoms produce heat as they split. The heat warms water. A machine called a steam generator turns the water to steam. The steam powers four motors called turbines. The turbines turn propellers located at the rear of the ship. These rotating blades also are called screws. The propellers move the carrier through the water.

Nuclear Power

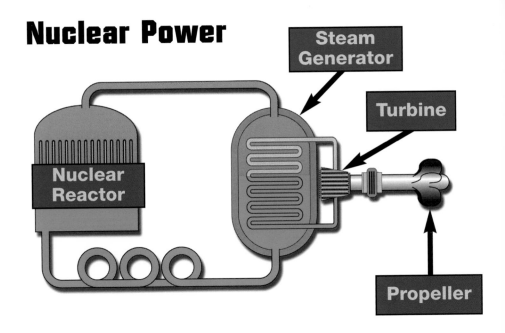

Weapons

Aircraft are supercarriers' most important weapons. But sailors on supercarriers use other weapons. *Nimitz*-class carriers have missiles called Sea Sparrows. These missiles can destroy enemy missiles before they reach the battle group. Radar equipment guides Sea Sparrows to their targets.

Some supercarriers have the Phalanx Close-In Weapons System. This system uses

Supercarriers sometimes fire Sea Sparrow missiles.

radar equipment to detect enemy aircraft or missiles that are close to the battle group. The system includes a machine gun that quickly fires ammunition.

Safety
Supercarriers are built to be safe. The Navy uses strong steel to build many ship parts. The steel helps reduce damage from enemy weapons.

Supercarriers also have equipment to control fires. Supercarriers have water sprinklers that turn on when they detect smoke or fire. The ships also have fire plugs. Water flows through the plugs and into hoses. Crewmembers then can use the hoses to direct water at a fire. Steel doors called bulkheads help prevent a fire from spreading throughout the ships.

A carrier's flight deck can be dangerous for crewmembers. Aircraft create dangerous conditions as they take off and land. The strong winds aircraft create could blow someone off the deck. Safety nets hang along the edge of the flight deck. These nets are there to catch anyone who falls overboard. Crewmembers on the flight deck also wear life jackets.

The flight deck and other open areas on supercarriers often become wet from ocean water or rain. The floors of these open areas are covered with a special coating to make them less slippery. It helps prevent crewmembers from falling or sliding off the deck.

Carriers use water from the ocean. Ocean water contains a great deal of salt. It is not safe for people to drink. But a filtration system on supercarriers removes the salt from the ocean water. Sailors use this fresh water for drinking, cooking, and washing. A supercarrier may produce about 400,000 gallons (1.5 million liters) of fresh water each day.

Crewmembers on supercarriers have equipment to protect themselves if a fire occurs.

Island

Flight Deck

Hull

Bow

Chapter Four

Supercarriers at Sea

Naval battle groups sail to many parts of the world. Trained crewmembers live on the ships for long periods of time. They always are prepared to carry out important missions.

Training

The men and women who serve in the U.S. Navy are volunteers. They choose to join the military. Some Navy members receive basic training. These people are called seamen recruits. They take classes and perform physical tests during basic training. Seamen recruits are called seamen apprentices after basic training.

Some supercarrier crewmembers help pilots take off and land safely on the flight deck.

Navy members who want to sail on a ship receive extra training. They become skilled in running one part of the ship. They also learn how to fight fires and repair ships.

Air wing pilots also receive special training. People who want to fly Navy aircraft must be college graduates and be officers in the Navy. Officers have more training and education than other Navy members.

Navy pilots train at various training airfields. They first learn to fly small aircraft. The pilots then fly larger, more powerful aircraft. Navy pilots train for about two years before they serve on a carrier.

The Battle Group

Supercarriers travel in the center of battle groups. Different types of ships travel around supercarriers. One type of battle group ship is a guided missile cruiser. Cruisers can fire missiles at ships, aircraft, or land targets.

Guided missile cruisers have a defense system called the Aegis Anti-Air Warfare System. The Aegis system uses computers and radar to track

Destroyers often sail in battle groups.

Supercarriers travel in the center of battle groups.

distant objects. It can guide missiles as they travel toward enemy targets.

A battle group also has destroyers and frigates. Destroyers fire guided missiles. Many destroyers also have an Aegis Anti-Air Warfare System. Frigates hunt and attack enemy submarines. Some destroyers also perform this mission.

Some battle groups have submarines. These ships have weapons to attack other submarines and warships. They also can fire missiles at land targets.

Carriers sometimes meet supply ships at sea. The supply ships bring food, fuel, weapons, and other supplies. These supplies allow the carriers to stay at sea for longer periods of time.

Supercarriers at Work

Navy supercarriers are based on the eastern and western coasts of the United States. The main eastern port is in Norfolk, Virginia. Western ports include San Diego in California and Washington's Everett and Bremerton ports.

Carriers are forward deployed for six months at a time. This term means that they are ready for combat. Two or three battle groups throughout the world usually are forward deployed at one time. If an emergency situation arises, the closest battle group can quickly reach the area.

Carriers are cleaned and repaired after about three years of service. Maintenance crews sometimes add new electronic systems or weapons to these supercarriers.

The Navy works hard to maintain its supercarriers. These ships are valuable to the U.S. military. They will continue to protect the United States and other countries in times of need.

Supercarriers sometimes come to shore for maintenance.

Words to Know

air wing (AIR WING)—the aircraft, pilots, and technicians on a carrier

arresting wire (uh-REST-ing WIRE)—a wire on a flight deck of a carrier that helps landing aircraft stop quickly

bulkhead (BUHLK-head)—a wall that separates areas inside a ship; bulkheads help prevent fires from spreading throughout a ship.

catapult (KAT-uh-puhlt)—a device that launches aircraft off the flight deck

island (EYE-luhnd)—the area on a carrier's flight deck where the captain and crew operate the ship

propeller (pruh-PEL-ur)—a set of rotating blades that provides force to move a ship through water

turbine (TUR-bine)—a motor that turns a propeller on a supercarrier

To Learn More

Bennett, Christopher. *Supercarrier.*
Enthusiast Color. Osceola, Wis.:
Motorbooks International, 1996.

Green, Michael. *Aircraft Carriers.* Land
and Sea. Mankato, Minn.: Capstone
High-Interest Books, 1998.

Green, Michael. *The United States Navy.*
Serving Your Country. Mankato, Minn.:
Capstone High-Interest Books, 1998.

Holmes, Tony. *Combat Carriers: Flying
Action on Carriers at Sea.* Osceola, Wis.:
Motorbooks International, 1998.

Useful Addresses

National Museum of Naval Aviation
1750 Radford Boulevard
Suite C
Pensacola, FL 32508

Naval Historical Center
Washington Navy Yard
805 Kidder Breese SE
Washington, DC 20374-5060

Naval Undersea Museum
610 Dowell Street
Keyport, WA 98345

USS Forrestal Museum
P.O. Box 59
West River, MD 20778

Internet Sites

The Carriers
http://www.chinfo.navy.mil/navpalib/ships/
   carriers

Home of the Aircraft Carrier
http://www.hq.navy.mil/airwarfare/N885/n885
   _home.htm

Nova Online—Battle Alert in the Gulf
http://www.pbs.org/wgbh/nova/battlegroup

The United States Navy
http://www.navy.mil

Index